FOREWORD

When one becomes a life coach following a certification program, the common advice is to solve practical problems for the people around you. Out of the myriad of practical problems in the world, I decided to tackle procrastination because at the time I, myself, was dealing with procrastinations of my own. Starting a new business as a life coach, I had so many administrative tasks and client-facing work to do and I noticed myself delaying those actions multiple times. In general I always like to self-coach on an issue before working with a client on it, so I summarized my approach on procrastination on my first pdf to give to potential clients who sign up to my email list.

At the time, I defined procrastination as a brain issue. The unmanaged, hyperactive primitive brain struggling against the underdeveloped, passive prefrontal cortex - that framing made sense to me. However, because people are usually interested in just solving their problems instead of learning about their brain, I wanted to develop something more practical - and that gave birth to the second pdf I provided to my readers, *The Anti-Procrastination Brain Recipes*. I framed procrastination as a result of a "messy kitchen", so to speak- and provided ways of cleaning up the kitchen and inviting more appetizing thoughts to come so you can do the action of making the food.

But for some reason I knew that I wasn't done telling the story of procrastination. By this time I had worked with multiple clients on procrastination issues and noticed that there is an underlying formula to the grand topic of "action". Procrastination was one of the outcomes of the action formula and depending on the parameters of this formula, there were other outcomes. The most significant part about this discovery was the possibility that everybody can willfully change parts of their formula to produce their desired outcome, because their current outcome is already following the formula. In other words, the problem behavior that people call "procrastination" was the result of their internal action formula working as intended.

I am a big believer of unshaming and viewing everyone as a complete, whole person at any point in their adult life. I want you to know that what you call "procrastination", and how that means you're a problematic person, is just one way to view your multifaceted life. I want to give you another view, a view that recognizes your whole intelligence. This book offers you a new way to view how you think about your action and I think with this knowledge you can make everything easy. No need for forced motivation, no need to wait for inspiration, no need for strict discipline - everything can be effortless.

TIPS FOR USING THIS BOOK

Have Fun

Let's talk a bit more about the effortless part. Picture this. At the end of your day, you lie down on your bed and turn off the lights. As you blink a few times and close your eyes, you feel your eyes relaxing as it now has nothing to focus on after a long day of looking at things. As your sense of vision takes a rest, your ears also note the silence in the room. Huh. The day was filled with lots of different sounds, but now even your ears are relaxing. As you lay still, inviting sleep into you, there's one thing that starts talking back to you: your brain.

"What did I even do today? Why didn't I do that thing? Why do I keep delaying that? Gah, I wish I could just finish that."

As this kind of conversation repeats day after day because you don't do the action you have in your mind, the tendency is to think of drastic measures to start doing the thing. We need a grand plan. We have to really make a big commitment and seriously put a lot of effort into making this change. The side effect of this is that it makes the change THAT much daunting, scary, and overwhelming - and that extends the cycle of inaction.

Now, I want to ask you this. Who says that change has to be drastic and hard? Who says that only the grindy kind of action is good, everything has to be tons of effort, and you need discipline? Well, actually plenty of people say that (including our parents, ha!) but who's to say that they are the authority in action? There is no golden rule or standard when it comes to human behavior, everyone can exercise free will and live their life on their terms.

Society likes to attribute success and deserving success to the grind, to the effort, to the discipline- but that's not the only way to view actions.

I want to offer you the possibility that we can have a lot of fun inviting more action into our lives. I'm not going to give you techniques to plan your day, ways to establish a habit in action, or how to think about motivation so that you can be motivated all the time. There are plenty of other books that do that, and if those worked well for you then I don't think you would have picked this book up. This book is all about fun, effortless action and when you understand the formula, you will see how that's possible for your life too. So as you continue on, I just want you to tell yourself: let's have fun doing things. That's the attitude I'm writing this book with, and I hope the energy conveys to you, the reader.

Trust Yourself (~)

The common thread that ties all symptoms of weak mental health is not trusting yourself to make the right decisions about your life. So many times we are placed in a dilemma or a fork in the road because we don't know which one is the right choice for us. We like to shame ourselves and "whip" ourselves into shape, so to speak, because we believe without that kind of pressure we would ruin ourselves to oblivion. Before you really dive into this book I want to plant the seed of a very important idea in your mind: your life is being piloted by the most perfect person to live your life, you. You always make the best decisions for yourself with the knowledge you have at the time, and you literally cannot mess up your life.

Let's say you have a regret about your past. You think that by making the wrong move or wrong choice you messed up your life. Therefore you are worthy of blame and you can't be trusted to make future decisions about your life. This is a common scenario that a lot of people can relate to, whether it be college choices, relationship choices, career choices, or family choices among others. But if you rewind time back to the time of the event...

Did you know that by acting that way you would cause the follow up events that transpired? No. We can't know, because we can't predict the future.

Even if you did know what was going to happen, that is just one possible outcome out of infinite possibilities in reality. Taking a more specific example, you may regret not taking a job offer because when you say no to a job offer you know you can't work there. But what if that company dissolved if you had taken the job offer? What if that company acquires your current company and you end up working there anyway? What if the new job completely ruined your work/life balance and you end up hating your life? These are all things that actually happen to people, but we only like to compare our current reality to the best possible hypothetical alternative.

You *never, ever* make a sub-optimal decision intentionally. That's just not what your brain does. Even if to some people your choices seem sub-optimal, to you there is an intelligent reason for making that choice. Since you live your life, it is important to you to follow up on that choice. We will talk more about this concept later, but every time you act upon something and you get to face the consequences of that action you learn something meaningful about that action, and that propels your life to a more informed direction.

We get stuck in life because we don't feed our brains new information that can break us out of our optimized decision making process. When we think we *have* to prioritize our parents' happiness before us, you will have to constantly give up your individuality and that will make you feel stuck in life. But when we learn that your parents are responsible for their own happiness and you don't owe them anything regardless of how much they say you do - you become more informed about how you can start living for yourself. This book is meant to be a guide in feeding new information about **action**. Trust your innate superpower of always making the perfect decisions for yourself and propel your life forward with that confidence.

As you read this book you will learn about so many instances when we do not give ourselves the authority and the permission to trust our intelligent selves. This subchapter is affixed with (~), and that symbol will recur throughout the book when this theme presents itself.

THE FORMULA

The premise of the action formula is that action is the output of a formula. The formula in simple terms being, action = your desire to do something - your unwillingness to do something. Sounds pretty simple and insignificant, right? If you want to do something more than you want to not do something, you'll do it and vice versa. This already gives us an insight: procrastination or inaction indicates that there is a greater unwillingness compared to the desire.

What happens if the opposite is true? Is begrudgingly doing something the same as doing something with joy, because in the end something is being done? What's the difference between something you genuinely have no desire to do versus something you feel bad about not doing? Those are the nuances that are explained with the full formula.

DEFINITION

Here is the definition of the formula:

$$A = D^{\wedge}H / P - (1+U)$$

Woah! Bunch of letters and symbols. Before you get overwhelmed, I promise you this isn't as complicated as it looks. Going over the letters first:

- A = action. Basically, the higher this value is the more effortless your actions become and the more negative this value is the more it is an energy sink for you.

- D = desire. Your desire to do something. Playing games is fun! Watching netflix is entertaining! Playing board games with friends is nice! All actions have some element of niceness to it, and that is what attributes to the desire to do those actions.

- H = hype. Now, we all know games are fun but let's say a new Pokemon game came out and you just finished downloading it onto your console. You can already feel the excitement as you load up the game, and you can't wait to meet your starter Pokemon. If you're not the gaming type, eating nice food is good but that restaurant reservation you made 2 months ago is coming and everyone says that that restaurant is the experience of a lifetime. The feeling that you get from these scenarios is hype.

- P = perfectionism, or pressure. If you're the type of person who thinks there's a difference between doing something vs. doing something WELL, then you have the pleasure of knowing perfectionism firsthand. Perfectionism is sort of a double edged sword; when applied effectively you can improve the quality of your output, but at the same time it does hinder your action and make it difficult to flow out of you effortlessly.

- U = unwillingness. We all have to do the dishes and vacuum our rooms but... it's so tedious... Doing the taxes, walking your dog on a rainy day, there are tons of reasons to not want to do something. Unwillingness is simply the opposite of desire.

- G = guilt, or shame. Guilt and shame associated with the unwillingness is the real killer of action. What's worse is, if you start feeling guilt and shame around your inaction - then you're not doing it and suffering at the same time. "I should study if I want better grades but..." "I haven't worked on my art in a week, I'm such a failure..." These types of judgmental feelings around your action is guilt and shame.

See? It's not too complicated. But why the math symbols? If you're well versed in math terminology, you'll probably understand the nuance of each element in the formula. Basically what the formula is saying is **hype exponentially increases the desire to do something, while perfectionism divides the desire. Guilt and shame multiplies the unwillingness to do the action.** In plain English, that's all there is to it.

THE RANGE OF A

Positive A

Numbers can be negative and positive. So what does a positive A value mean, and what does a negative A value mean? What does a 0 value mean? Any positive A means action is being done because the desire is greater than the unwillingness. But if the magnitude of A isn't *that* great, it probably means that the desire isn't all that big to begin with or the unwillingness is taking a big chunk out of the big desire. Speaking numerically, it's either 1 - 0 or 100 - 99; the result is 1 in the end. In real life terms, these are probably things you do out of necessity like chores or busywork. You don't really want to do them but at the same time if you don't do them you dig yourself into a bad hole so you begrudgingly do it.

I believe most people do actions in this fashion, and that's why action is so difficult to sustain. It's like you're pressing the gas pedal AND the brake on your car at the same time. Your car *does* move, but it makes loud sounds and damages the car in the process. When you do that for a while the car will be damaged and it will have to go to the shop. Something like that also happens in your brain. When your desire and unwillingness are constantly fighting, the battleground is your mind and the longer the battle goes on, the more fatigued the mind becomes.

People look for solutions to the problem where action is so hard to do, and the solution usually has to do with discipline, motivation, or consistency. Maybe drive and grit, too. But all of those things aren't addressing the core issue of WHY the action is hard but instead focuses on how to think differently about the difficulty. That is a sound approach and does use the mind's power to see things from a different perspective, but it doesn't change the source of the difficulty, namely the internal struggle between desire and unwillingness.

Grand A

Now, what if the desire is significantly big, and the unwillingness is small? That is the only way we can have a large value of A. When that happens, how is that different from a small value of A? Let's think of a realistic example. If you've been in a relationship, you probably remember days where you just can't wait to get off of work to meet your significant other. If you're a gamer, you may have fond memories of playing a game on your console or computer throughout the night when everybody else is sound asleep. If you're passionate about sports or art, you probably practiced and worked on your craft even when nobody asked you to. This is **effortless action** and how I want you to approach every action.

My father is a hypnotherapist in Korea and when I was in college I part-timed in his business as a desk clerk. There were countless parents who came in with their children, complaining to my father that their child was bad at studying because they're undisciplined and have poor concentration. My father would always argue that no, actually your child DOES have discipline and concentration; they probably don't want to apply that to studying because they don't find it fun enough. Then my father would ask the child, do you play video games? Can you play for hours and hours if your parents don't stop you? And nine times out of ten, they nod yes with a shy smile on their face.

The power to concentrate on something for hours and the power to consistently put effort into something already resides within you, but that power can only be harnessed when your feelings work together. Think of an action you loved doing and did effortlessly. Now, think of a situation where that action was frowned upon or judged. "Oh, you're going on dates instead of working over hours? How lazy is this generation, tsk tsk!". "Son, are you seriously playing on your computer as soon as you get back from school?" "You're a ballet dancer? Wow, can you really be financially successful with that? Good luck!" Can't you just feel the drive spiraling down? Unhindered, passionate desire is our key to unlocking effortless action and in the later chapters we're going to learn how to let nothing get in the way of your actions.

Zero A

What happens when A is zero? That happens when your desire to do something and unwillingness completely cancel each other out, or when they're both zero. An example of the former is considering a new hobby.

Can I try rock climbing? That sounds vaguely fun but it probably involves a lot of new equipment… I don't want to try it *that* much so let's look at another hobby. Perhaps swimming? Swimming does sound fun but I'm a bit self conscious with how I look in swimming suits so I don't really like that…

There is some desire to try the action but it's not enough to convince the unwillingness into action. The key point in a zero action value is that there is no lingering about the action. It's a **clean break**. It's like me potentially learning the flute or learning a Morocco-specific dialect of Arabic; while both are perfectly good for other people I genuinely have no interest in learning them. The easiest way to achieve this clean break is to not have any guilt associated with your unwillingness, because mathematically anything multiplied by zero is zero. Wow, isn't that cool?

Negative A

What starts happening when A goes below zero? Zero action already means nothing is getting done, so how is negative action possible? I define negative action as an energy sink, where you don't do the action but still expend energy not doing it. Think of not working on your final project for days and spending so much time and energy thinking you should do it. Maybe calling your parents more often. Maybe starting that diet or workout plan.

Everything that you DON'T do, and yet actively spend energy as if you WERE doing is the result of a negative A.

Mathematically, this means the unwillingness to do something is larger than the desire to do it. Just like how hype is the amplifier for desire, guilt and shame is the amplifier of unwillingness and having guilt and shame around your inaction is the recipe for energy sinks. This is also the realm where procrastination happens, and my goal is to have you decide on a clean break from the action (zero A) instead of constantly having to spend energy on the procrastination sink.

SPECIAL MENTION: WAITING

Many people choose to not act because they're waiting for something. Waiting for inspiration to come, waiting for an event to happen, waiting for the right moment for something... Waiting is attractive to the mind and has a tangible benefit: **you don't have to do anything**. The world is going to solve your life problems for you. And if you're not motivated at the right time, you have to really grind to get your work done but when you are inspired and motivated, it becomes so much easier than waiting.

Makes sense, right? Because the time spent waiting for that inspiration is going to pay off a lot better than not feeling inspired and grinding through. So why don't we all just wait? Why do some people like to take action?

We all are free human beings with free individual will. You want to exercise that freedom in your consciousness. That's the whole reason why the history of humanity has evolved from a hierarchical system where the upper class imposes rules upon the lower class and then now and time went by and those systems crumbled. And some are even in the process of being crumbled right now to a state where a lot more people have free will. And waiting is partly just giving up that free will because you are at the effect of the world.

So when you're waiting for some big life event to happen to make you happy, it's practically the same as another really big large being in the skies, telling you that nothing you do matters until a point where I decide to give you something.

The benefit of not having to do anything comes at the cost of your free will. Being subject to this abstract entity that gives you what you're waiting for at the end. But in my experience, the root of most psychological problems come from an extended period of being subject to this kind of relationship with the world.

My history with depression was really, really intensified when I started realizing that nothing I do in this company is making any impact. But because of my green card status, I needed to stay at this company. So I'm working at this job, and it's not like I'm not getting paid; but everything that I do just ends up not mattering. And that was extremely unmotivating for me. And as weeks and months of that happened on and on and on, I just slowly lost all will to do anything in life. So this may be your experience too.

My strong opinion is that all human brains are equipped with this executive functioning brain and this executive functioning brain wants to go out into the world, wants to leave its footprints and express itself out into the world. And when that dream is continuously suppressed, then the mind becomes weakened. And when the mind is weak and it becomes ill and it cannot function as well when it actually wants to function, it's like not having worked out in the years and then suddenly you're forced to go to a marathon. You can't.

Waiting for big, good, and important things to happen is a big chapter in the story of my life. When you go look at my website, I have this whole story about it where I'm in high school and I'm thinking, "if only I was in college". Then I go to college and now I think, " if only I graduated". Then I got out of undergrad to transition to "I only I had a masters degree" which then transpired to "if only I was out of the army"…

It keeps on going. I got out of the Army and I thought "if only I had a job in America", then when I got a job I thought " if only I had a green card". Now, that whole process was about 20 years and when I finally got my green card… I realized there was nothing on the other side. I just kept on waiting and waiting and waiting because I thought some next big great thing was going to automatically make me happy.

What I wasn't really realizing at the time is I had all the agency in myself to start making myself happy, regardless of the external consequences. To be honest, I didn't think like that because inside of me was this lack of appreciation for myself. Yes, of course I could work hard and I could try to make myself happy right now, but is it worth it?

Am I really worth that?

That has been the underlying thought behind all of my passive waiting.

Now, I wrote about my life for a few paragraphs because I have a greater point to make. An interesting aspect of waiting is *romantic* waiting. You're trying to be the love interest of someone and you're waiting for the courage to text them, then you're waiting for them to contact you back. *That* kind of waiting.

But when you're looking at your phone impatiently during that waiting period, while it can feel very torturous it can also make you understand and appreciate the **desire** – how much you desire this other party.

Seen in this perspective, you're *romantic* waiting for this good thing in your life that will come after this grueling waiting experience. So what is it? What comes out of the waiting is your future self. The fact that you're willing to wait *this* much for your future self tells you how much you value your future self.

Because if you knew that this "future you" wasn't that great, then you wouldn't bother waiting for it. If you walk into a cafe and they make you wait 36 hours for an espresso, no matter how much you enjoy coffee you're probably not going to wait that long. It is not *that* valuable to you. But you wait for great things to happen in your life because *you* value *your life* underneath. You just haven't aligned yourself with that notion of valuing yourself enough to start taking action today.

With the information you get from the upcoming chapters, you will think of small actions you can take today for the most valuable person in your life, you.

THE ACTION ENSEMBLE

If you're in STEM and can understand the mathematical notations, the formula probably makes a lot of sense to you now. But in case you're not fond of math, I present to you the action ensemble.

I worked with artist Riri Flawyi (https://twitter.com/ririflawyi) to have characters created for each part of the formula. Giving identity and personality to our feelings is a powerful way to think about the self because it takes advantage of our creativity. We are human beings with brains, not single state machines like computers. We have the capability to feel emotions at will, in fact - multiple emotions at will. We can feel hungry while we're eating. We can feel lonely while inside a group of friends. We can love and feel resentful at the same time. These are powerful human moments that are possible because of our brain's capability to feel multiple emotions at the same time.

This idea was explored in the Pixar film Inside Out (2015). If you saw the film you probably tried out thinking like this, perhaps visualizing what each of your feelings would look like. The advantage of separating feelings like this is we get to exercise seeing the same thing from multiple angles. Let's use an example to illustrate this point.

Say you're about to go for a job search but looking at all the job applications and filling out all the forms is so intimidating. And each time you submit a resume you have to customize it to the company you're applying to and you're also writing a cover letter as well. On top of that you have bills to pay and the job search hasn't been going well for the past few months. Sounds like a pretty common bad situation, right?

When you don't apply to jobs in this situation, the blockers in this situation are the unwillingness because filling out forms generally suck, and guilt/shame because you're not doing the things you should be doing. So by default you believe YOU are lazy and YOU are preventing yourself from getting a job, and that's where I want to offer you this alternative thought: we confuse what we think vs. what our FEELING thinks.

There is a difference between YOU not wanting to do it vs. your UNWILLINGNESS not wanting to do it. YOU are the executive leader of individual feelings each with its own trait and characteristics. YOU have the ability to listen to every feeling and collect their inputs and have a final say on what you want to do. From the above example, your unwillingness doesn't want to do the busywork of filling out forms and applying to jobs and your guilt/shame is saying horrible things about yourself. But what does desire have to say about this situation?

Desire probably really wants a nice, well-paying job you deserve that can pay the bills and give you some more money to save up and occasionally splurge on. Desire probably wants to prove itself by providing professional labor in exchange for money. Desire probably wants to get this over with. Desire has lots of ideas on why you WANT to do the job search in the first place.

What can hype add to this situation? Hype offers you how great it would feel to finally land that offer letter and throw a celebration. Hype gives you a preview of how you're going to be the top contributor to your new company. Hype tells you all the wonderful professionals you're going to meet in the interview process. Perfectionism can offer its ideas too, about how resumes should look professional and cover letters should sound genuine and such.

Just by evaluating what each feeling would think, YOU at the top have a more comprehensive view of the situation compared to before. With this comprehensive view you see that it is not that YOU are lazy and self-sabotaging, but rather you have the desire to get a nice, well-paying job but your unwillingness feels like it is tedious. This opens up further explorations like is the desire okay with stopping the job search? How about if we don't customize each resume and cover letter?

So with that, let me re-introduce the action formula, but this time with personality and characteristics.

DESIRE

Desire is our wonderful protagonist who is amped up to try everything. Desire is the part of us who never grew up from the constantly curious, constantly wondering, and constantly fun days of our youth. Desire never turns away from anything at first sight because desire ALWAYS wants to at least do something first. You probably were very close to desire when you were young but other characters started having a more prominent voice in your life. But they never left you, they're still inside looking for the next exciting thing to try.

For life in general desire is one of many characters inside of you but for action desire is the main protagonist. Your story of action is one of desire successfully going through something despite the hardships and difficulties. Not everything that desire wants to do will be easy, and desire will need some friends and allies to help them while not being discouraged by enemies; it is your job as the director of your life to unfold desire's journey.

Here are some questions I use to assess if desire is present in this action.

1. Am I doing this action for me? Or for someone else?
2. Is there a joy or fun I can find in this action?
3. Do I have to do this action or would I not do it if I had the choice?

Wide Interest Vs. Narrow Focus

Because desire loves everything and wants to do everything, there is a side effect of everything looking attractive. When you're working on one thing, another thing looks attractive and as you switch suddenly ANOTHER thing looks attractive. This is largely seen as a liability in society and is labeled lacking attention. When this aspect of desire is curtailed it won't just make desire focus on one thing but rather it will discourage desire completely.

At a buffet you have a wide array of dishes to choose from. Imagine someone criticizing you for eating a plate full of different food at a buffet. Criticizing yourself for having a wide interest is as nonsensical as being forced to eat only mashed potatoes at a buffet. Each time we're interested and attracted to the idea of doing something, that desire springs from something inside of us that feels an affinity towards that activity. That affinity may come from a childhood dream or a natural penchant. The affinity may be you trying to fill a void in your life. No matter what the reason is, it is an intelligent one that is trying to serve you.

At the same time, when you're trying to meet a deadline for your project but suddenly find yourself extremely drawn to shopping for rock climbing equipment, the wide interest is not helpful for you at that moment. So we can benefit from a way to manage the wide interest in times when we need a narrow focus. For that I recommend the methodology I call The Side Dish Practice.

The Side Dish Practice
1. Pick one activity that is separate from the primary activity. If you have multiple, you will switch between them.
2. Work on the primary activity until the desire for the side activity is unbearable, then switch to the side activity.
3. **Without judgment on yourself**, fully immerse yourself in the side activity until the desire to work on

---

the primary activity becomes unbearable.
4. Repeat step 2, switching the side activity as necessary.

The difficult parts about this activity are twofold.
One is there tends to be less of a desire to do the primary activity, especially if it is something that is assigned to you rather than something that you genuinely want to do without being told to do it. I'm writing this book out of a desire to share my knowledge with my readers. This is something that is not assigned to me, so it is relatively easy for me to do it. Doing a deep clean of the house to prepare for guests who are going to be staying at our place for a few weeks is something I would like to do for a happy marriage and happy guest hosting experience, but it is not something I really would prefer doing if I had the choice to not do it.
The other is that it is extremely challenging to not feel bad about fully immersing yourself in a distracting activity. (~) When I ask clients to commit to watching Netflix instead of doing it out of the discomfort of doing the primary activity, the most common response is that "if I did that I would literally watch twenty different series and would never get anything done". But the thing is, your brain is not designed for hours of the same kind of stimulus. Your brain is great at recognizing patterns and generalizing incoming stimuli. The first few episodes of a new series is going to be an intense dopamine hit, but the pacing of the show, how the characters act, when a suspense is built, when a twist comes - these are patterns that can be picked up by your brain with relative ease.
So many of us think we should be doing work and get distracted anyway, and then we feel bad about being distracted and put the task off again. Just like how when you focus on doing the work distractions seem very attractive, when you **fully commit** to your distractions it not only makes the primary work attractive but you actually get a lot of the entertainment / rest / distracting stimulations out of the way and it makes focusing on the primary task that much easier. I stand by this method no matter how many

people think it's weird; this method is how I play video games almost daily for multiple hours and yet get work for two jobs done. If you try this method as I outlined in the instructions, I'm confident you will find the same level of success as me.

HYPE

Frodo has Gandalf, Harry Potter has Dumbledore. Every young protagonist needs a wiser and more powerful superhero to give them the power to develop and break through hardships, and that's exactly who hype is. Think of hype as the overpowered superhero whose existence basically means every problem is solved. That truly is the case. With enough hype, anything can be effortless - even with unwillingness, guilt, and shame.

In superhero movies and comics the heroes usually have some weakness to make the stories interesting, but I want you to imagine hype as a hero who's so strong that they're kind of boring and uninteresting. Because with any action in your life, I can guarantee you you're not excited about the things that you aren't doing. Moreover with anything that you do effortlessly already, you probably have a lot of hype. It's really that simple.

Since we now know that everything takes care of itself when hype shows up, we just have to focus on HOW we're going to summon hype. Let's examine those techniques now.

How To Invite Hype

The concept of feelings can be vague but for the purposes of this chapter I use the word feeling for the physical aspect of it. When the emotion I'm experiencing is excitement, I **feel** certain things in my body. My heart beats faster. My face makes a smile. I get a bit jittery, almost as if I'm caffeinated. My body keeps making small, choppy movements. That is my physical experience of excitement, and that is what I mean when I say I'm feeling excited in this chapter.

Hype can be invited by reflecting upon previous experiences of hype and borrowing hype from the future. When have you felt hype before? Right before a big reveal of something you worked hard on? When you got a lot of praise for your performance? When you got first place in something? When you hear the word hype, if there was an experience that you specifically remember you can borrow hype from that past experience.

Just like I described excitement above, how would you describe your feeling hyped?

1. What does hype look like when you close your eyes?
    a. Is it a solid? Liquid? Gas? What shape does it have?
    b. What are its colors? Is it a solid color or a gradient?
    c. Does it move or is it static?
2. What sound does hype make inside your mind?
    a. Which ear do you hear hype in?
    b. What is the volume of hype?
    c. Is there a song that's playing?
3. Where does hype live in your body?
    a. What sensation are you feeling in your chest? Legs? Feet? Hands? Arms? Shoulders and neck? Face? Head? Belly?
    b. What is the temperature of that feeling?
    c. What is the texture of that feeling like?

4. What does hype smell like to you?
5. If you take a dip or bite, what does hype taste like?
6. Imagine your hype as a comic book strip or a scene from a movie. Describe it in detail.

Going through the five senses like this will explicitly define the experience of hype. If you're not really sure, the trick is to vividly remember all the details about the event that made you have the emotional reaction. What faces were other people making? Slow down the frame rate and play the video of your hype in slow motion and take note of all the details in the scene. This will amplify the experience.

You can also borrow from the future, and I personally believe this is the more fun out of the two because this helps you define specific outputs of the action you want to feel excited about.

What comes out as a result of your activity? What is the specific, tangible result you get? If you want to feel excited about your job search, imagine looking at your bank account with a regularly scheduled deposit and see how that number increases over time. That's a specific and tangible result. If you want to feel excited about your academics, imagine receiving congratulations from your dean as they shake your hand and give you your diploma on graduation day. You get to write on your resume what degree you have, and in the higher education section you get to select a different option. Depending on the country you live in and the industry, having that degree will be a factor in jobs literally opening their doors to you. So many recruiters piling up on your inbox asking for your interest... That is a specific and tangible result.

As you imagine that and repeat the hype-feeling process from above... you will be able to borrow hype from the future. When you're fully embodying it by describing it and feeling it, you will observe your actions in a different manner. That is when action is going to effortlessly flow out of you.

Getting Success From the Action

The process I described above is all about actions you haven't done yet. In the end the goal of this book is to get you to actually do the actions. The good news here is that when you actually do the work and you gain success as a result, you become a perpetual motion machine; the hype you get from the achievement will further fuel action. Not only do you get hype, but repeated action will also increase your proficiency in doing the same action so you will get more done in the same amount of time or the quality of your output will increase given the same amount of effort.

A more important side effect of getting something done has to do with self love. Imagine as a kid wanting to have a bicycle. Your parents keep saying that they will buy you a bike, but they never follow through on that promise. When that happens, you're bound to feel some disappointment as a child. Say you live with a significant other and they keep saying they will do the chores, wash the dishes, vacuum the house - but they never do. They say they love you, but they never show it in action. It becomes difficult for what they say to be credible.

Not doing anything in and of itself is fine. There is nothing requiring you to do anything in this world. The universe's action police are not going to pursue you if you don't do anything. But doing something for yourself is a powerful demonstration of self-love. In this world, where you don't have to do anything, you are doing something for yourself. Isn't that powerful? You're like the protagonist in a romantic movie, overcoming the rain, delayed trains, and other obstacles to show you your love.

Hype From Places

Muslims can pray from anywhere, but they seek to visit Mecca at least once in their lifetime. Martial artists from across the world hope to visit and train at Japan's Budokan. Studying can be done from anywhere but college students choose to go to libraries. Why is that? While actions can be done from anywhere, some places are better equipped for the task than others and more importantly some places have more inviting energy for certain actions. The distinct energy that comes from a place can be used to your advantage when it comes to action.

For example I describe a cafe. Cafes are a wonderful hub for various activities. People hold social activities, some people like to read in solitude, and others plan their entrepreneurial journey all inside a cafe. As I describe this scene you can already visualize people engaged in their activities. Just looking at other people engaged in their action can be a great invitation to *your* action because observing them can trigger your unconscious mirroring. When you occupy the same space as them the unconscious mirroring and the collective energy of the place will bleed into you, generating hype.

So many people understand that when trying to exercise regularly, the exercise itself is fairly easy once you get to the gym; it's getting to the gym that is difficult. We'll discuss how to address that part in the next section, but take from that example and try thinking about the most appropriate place for your planned activities. Making the trip to that location already is a form of action, and by getting there you start the chain reaction of action because the location you arrived at will be inviting to the activity.

On Disappointment

In general feeling hype is good and all, but many of you may be used to not feeling excited because it is closely associated with the experience of being let down and disappointed. The amount of disappointment is proportional to the amount of excitement you have and we typically try to minimize the disappointment by minimizing our excitement. I am generalizing to excitement because this chapter is about hype, but this also applies to our desires as well. The more we want, the more likely we are to be disappointed. I want to blow your mind a little bit and tell you that it is completely possible to feel desire / excitement without any possibility of disappointment.

This is possible because disappointment is not attached to your desire or excitement. The disappointment is attached to your need to control things that are outside of you.

Suppose you want to ask someone out on a date. You excite yourself for it and muster up the courage to ask them out, only to be rejected. This can be a disappointing experience that deters you from any future interactions. But what causes the disappointment? It is the expectation of them reciprocating your feelings. If you are disappointed, you have this expectation whether you are conscious of it or not. You cannot control the other person's behavior but you expect them to follow your expectations and when they prove that they are outside of your control, that's when disappointment comes in.

Wanting your partner to change causes pain because they will not. Wanting a company to hire you causes pain because they hold the power to hire you. The want is separate from what is being wanted, and in this case the wanted thing has brought us disappointment.

Then you might be wondering about what about things I can control? I still get disappointed when I don't reach my goals. Say your goal is to make one million dollars. Wanting that money to come to you magically... is wanting things that are outside of your control. So what do you have to do in order to make a million dollars? Asking again, what do you have to do in order to make a million dollars? When the focus is on you, it gives you more of an actionable mindset to make it happen for yourself.

Even then, you may fail along the way. What stops you from getting up and tells you that you're disappointed? It's shame. Shame is the internalized voice of oppression and societal pressure. "You should have a home by age xy!", "If you don't work at Fortune 500 companies, why do you even live?", "How dare you treat a rich person like that, when you're so poor!" are some of the things the shaming voice says. When shame is internalized, it wears the guise of you so you may think it is you who still feels disappointed.

To truly live a life that you want, you have to stop wanting to control things that are outside of you. As long as you keep that ground rule, you can want to your heart's content and be scar-free. We'll learn more about tackling shame in the chapter for shame.

It does not take a ton of success to get this powerhouse started, but it does take something to get started. Even with hype you may struggle with starting your action because of the next character we will meet, perfectionism. I have tips on how to redefine your relationship with this character, so let's keep going.

PERFECTIONISM

Perfectionism is that overly picky military officer who will find the smallest spec of dust in the camp and give every troop 20 push-ups for punishment. Or that DMV worker who sends you to the back of the line because you forgot to fill out one blank in your form. Or that chef who throws away everything he made for an hour because the dish isn't "right". Perfectionism believes that there isn't just a way to do things, but a "right" way to do things.

As you can probably imagine, perfectionism really slows down action because it doesn't want to settle for "okay". It wants the process of the action to be perfect and the result of the action to be perfect, otherwise it's worthless. As such perfectionism and shame/guilt really "get" each other. But there is an admirable quality to perfectionism, and it is that it cares about what comes out of the action. Sometimes that extra cherry on top is the difference between a good dessert and a great dessert.

In desire's journey, perfectionism will sometimes be an ally and sometimes be an enemy. As the director we're going to learn to listen to the inner desires of perfectionism and communicate with them to make both desire and perfectionism feel satisfied. Desire is a wonderful protagonist and does not want to burn bridges and sour relationships just to make their dreams come true, and that is a theme that will recur in the upcoming character descriptions.

With perfectionism being a double edged sword, how do we manage it to invite more action into our lives? Do we lower our expectations and accept that we are not perfect? Do we just gaslight ourselves into believing that my five minute sketch is as good as my two month project?

Believably Small

> "OK. Starting tomorrow, I'm going to really change the way I eat."
> "On my next exam, I'm gonna study really hard and get an A."
> "Next time, I'm gonna make sure I do something for our anniversary."

These are some things I hear on a daily basis from many people around the internet. Sadly, the way that these things are said indicates almost certainly that these things are not going to be done.

Here's the bottom line: the majority of blocked action I see comes from the deadly mix of perfectionism and guilt. Examining each of the sentences above, on the surface level it looks like determination and will, almost a commitment to action. When peeled a few layers deeper, what it actually is hiding underneath is:

> "The way I eat is unacceptable and I'm a bad person for eating like this. Today is already ruined and tainted with my shitty diet; I'm gonna make sure starting tomorrow it is pure and good."
> "My current grade and how I didn't study indicates I'm stupid and lazy. Anything other than A is unacceptable and to be honest, trash. I'm gonna prove to myself that my life is worth something by getting that A next time, because as of right now - I'm worthless."
> "I fucked up on this anniversary by not remembering it and to be honest I just couldn't decide on something to do because I wanted to do something super grand for my spouse. This anniversary is already done but next time I'm gonna make sure that it is a special day".

The pattern I'm trying to solve for you is the shame around the way you are today and how tomorrow HAS to be 100% different. But why is this particular combination such a deadly mix?

29

Making pasta for one is vastly different from making pasta for 1000 people. If you've seen the short videos on this creator doubling the # of eggs in his pasta dough every attempt, you'll understand what I mean. But it's not just the same type of work, multiplied by 1000; when significant magnitude is involved, how you approach the problem has to be different. Specifically, it's not just a matter of kneading the dough for 1000 more times but how you portion the egg, the amount of work surface you need, the equipment required is all different. While it may look like the same problem, they're different types of problems.

In the realm of software engineering this topic is called scalability, and this is what makes Facebook and Twitter so hard to replace. Anybody can create a replica of Facebook for one person (literally, the core functionality can be developed by anyone); but doing it for the entire globe requires dedicated technology and hardware. So all this is to say, solving one problem is different from solving an entire set of problems no matter how similar the problems are to each other.

With that, let's go back to the earlier examples. Changing what you eat in a single plate is something you can do today. Maybe exchange the soda for water. Maybe portion your food onto one plate. Maybe leave food on the plate. These are all actions that can be taken in a single sitting, regardless of the day. But planning your whole meal plan, figuring out your ideal portions, balancing hydration in between, taking into account social interactions, and all of the above - this cannot be effectively changed in a single day. In terms of study habits, watching multiple tutorials in one topic you didn't fully understand is something you can do today. Looking at the course material and pre-portioning the amount to study for the week is doable. Setting up appointments with tutors and instructors is doable. Converting textbook material to digestible notes is doable. Study is a combination of all these things, and just because the clock is past 12 - doesn't mean you're going to be able to make ALL of those changes at once.

In romance, an appreciative talk is something you can do today. A rose for no reason, going on a walk together after dinner, watching the stars from the balcony, giving your spouse an extra long hug before bed are all expressions of love you can do today. If you're not used to expressing love in small, daily doses it's going to be very difficult to plan for a GRAND expression of love because all the steps that lead to the grand expressions are missing in the middle.

So by telling yourself that you're going to change at the NEXT opportunity... You're almost setting yourself up for the same pattern. Every time an action feels too big to do today so you want to do it tomorrow, chunk it down to something that is so believably small that you can act on it **today**.

Perfectionist Shame

As you could have imagined, perfectionism and shame go together very well. Perfectionism tends to invite shame because when we do something it is very unlikely that it will be perfect, and when it is not perfect we think it is worthless and we should be ashamed for not making it perfect. This can extend to feeling like blaming ourselves for not making perfect progress or not being perfect in the first place.

Shame enters our lives through other people's perspectives. To provide a simplified example, when we first draw with our crayons we have no way of knowing if our work is good or not, it just is our drawing. Through the eyes of approving or disapproving people we learn how to feel about our creations. When your parents are proud of you for drawing something and they put it on the fridge, your developing brain learns that doing things is fun and worth celebrating. But when your teacher looks at your drawing with a sigh and points out all the things that are "wrong " with it, you learn that trying something and not making it good is worthy of a sigh. Moreover, that sigh actually makes you feel pretty bad and your brain wants to make sure it never experiences that again! Not experiencing that bad feeling unfortunately comes at the cost of your joyful self-expression, and just like that a light inside of you dims.

Any time you try to make progress, perfectionism lays its eyes on you and tells you a hundred reasons why this is not the right way to make progress. When you finally get discouraged after a thousand disapproving glances, you give up and shame tells you how much of a failure you are because you couldn't even get that thing done. You've tried so many times you should have figured it out by now but you didn't. You suck.

Innate Perfection

Why do we still think this way in the first place? It's because we tend to think we aren't good enough today. Continuing the earlier examples of big changes, we should be ashamed of our diet, weight, and appearance. We should be ashamed of our grades, our academic standing, our financial status. We should be ashamed of how crappy romantic partners we are and how much we suck as human beings. The pressure you put on yourself is almost like a crucifixion; by putting yourself under this stress and pain, you absolve yourself of the SIN that you are.

If only you looked better... If only you lost some weight... If only you were smarter... If only you went to Oxford... If only you worked at Apple... If only you got your partner the most expensive diamond ring... You'd be able to feel good about yourself but you don't today - so you have to suffer... By suffering you remember WHY you're in this much suffering in the first place - it is because of your lack... So of course you deserve to suffer...

Because we aren't good enough today, the word "today" is already tainted. There was this wonderful canvas that contained today, and with my crappy self I've ruined that - so I need to work with a new canvas so that it can be wonderful, your brain says. Because we view ourselves so bad, we can't help but to want the polar opposite - something so complete and good. Partial good can't be good enough because it still contains traces of my crappy self. Bleh!

That is precisely the notion I'm trying to dismantle. You are already complete. (~) You are already perfect. Everything that you do, you do for an intelligent reason. There's nothing wrong with the way you are today. What you ate today is a perfect choice considering ease, cost, and deliciousness. How you studied for the last exam was the perfect choice of your desire to balance mental health, fun, relaxation, academic responsibilities and your interest in the topic. What you did for your spouse was your best expression of love to your capacity at the time - you weren't intentionally withholding while knowing how to express more. You already WERE living your perfect life today, you just didn't see it that way.

So not tomorrow, starting right now - you're going to continue to make informed best decisions about your life. With this chapter you now know that small actions lead up to big changes. Your brain is already thinking of ways to incorporate small changes in your life. Your brain understands it's okay to not be good at new things you try, because how the fuck can you be good at something you've never done before? Your brain appreciates its perfection today and sees perfection at what other people might call crappy. Why is this possible? Because that's what you always were - a capable, perfect, and complete person who uniquely bloomed in the form of you. Changes are going to come not because you SHOULD have those changes - but because you WANT those changes.

Everything Is Valuable and
Nothing Is Wasted

Because perfectionism is about doing things the "right" way or even the "perfect" way, we tend to face difficulties in action because we don't want to go the "wrong" way. This can be why we spend so much time trying to optimize our working environment or equipment prior to actually doing the work, because doing the work outside of optimal condition means the output is not going to be good and your effort becomes a waste.

If you are trying to market, you may be contemplating on which social platforms to run your ads on because you do not want to waste your money by making sub-optimal ad choices. You may be an aspiring software engineer trying to improve your portfolio. You want your portfolio to look good with the most popular types of open source projects so you may spend a lot of time trying to pick the right one. All of this time trying to make the right decisions to optimize value is time stolen away from actually taking action. The fact of the matter is, everything you do has value. By value I mean it gives your brain new information to update its auto-optimization neural network.

Applying this to the previous two examples, choosing any social network and running ads will still give you the experience of creating an ad campaign and defining how your campaign will run over the course of a time period. This kind of "busywork" not super related to ads is still part of running ads, and by choosing any platform and actually doing it you make your future ad creating processes more proficient. Moreover, when you transition into another platform you have something to actually compare against, so you *actually* know the difference between the platforms instead of just reading about the differences. For software engineering, coding is coding regardless of the project. What makes you write code and improve your coding is actually working on a project. Even if the project you choose does not become popular, the experience of writing code for that project translates over to future projects you will work on.

Image training and thinking about doing something is as beneficial as doing the action when it comes to performance, and that's evidenced by sports psychology. Since we are not brains in a jar, actually doing things has to have a different selling point compared to just thinking about it. The selling point is that your action now has a chance to interact with the world. Someone can see your output and think something about it. With that experience you achieve what the mind wants to do in this world: self-actualization. No matter how sub-optimal your action and its output may seem, it still creates the experience of self-actualization; and that is what truly matters in the grand scheme.

Actual Value vs. Perceived Value

In whatever you do, there is an outcome or a result. When you play the piano it makes sounds, when you draw you have a drawing at the end. When we repeat our actions and get more proficient at it, the quality of our outputs also change. With that you start getting reference points for comparison. How you used to draw can seem really bad compared to how you draw now. How you used to sing can sound horrible compared to how you sing now. When these kinds of comparisons start taking place in your mind you start idealizing the results that you haven't created yet and start comparing whatever you DO create to the ideal.

This kind of mindset puts you in a rut because nothing you do is good enough, and everything you do seems sub-par. But the thing is, you are not the ultimate judge in the quality of everything. If you think about it, even your standards change. As you get better at something, what you used to consider good also changes; if you were truly an ultimate judge of quality, shouldn't your standards be absolute and never change?

Think of your favorite foods. I can guarantee that not all of them are coming from Michelin star restaurants. In fact, some people may argue your favorite food is bad; but to you, it is delicious enough to be your favorite. How a person perceives value from something is almost completely independent of what the actual value of that thing is. The value of a bottle of ice cold water in a theme park would not be the same as that same bottle of water in a convenience store in Alaska.

Just because *you* feel like your work sucks does not mean that it *objectively* sucks. Every time you withhold yourself and stop yourself from creating action, you prevent someone who would find your work so valuable and life-changing. Not all of the most inspirational people in the world are #1 in their field. Sometimes people who do not even make it near the top of their field can be recognized for their resilience and character. You are just *one* judge of your work, and how rigged would the world be if one judge gets to make the call on everything?

Even if you create something that the world hates, that still has value because as discussed in the previous subchapter the process of creating that has given you repetitions in the skills and information about the creation process that you can re-use in the next attempt. The creation also may have its value changed the next day, just like how people changed their perception of Van Gogh's work after his death. Perfectionism gives you reasons to not do things today but none of those reasons deserve to stop your progress today.

UNWILLINGNESS

Unwillingness is just *sooooo* over it. Desire's enthusiastic energy is mirrored by unwillingness in the opposite direction. Something new to do? They can already think of 10 reasons why not to do it. Something you tried before? They have a list of reasons why not to do them ready to read. No matter what the possibilities are, unwillingness just doesn't want to do it.

Similar to how desire has the tendency to be sidetracked by everything because everything looks fun, unwillingness has the tendency to be always discontent and stressed. Because while they don't want to do anything, they also don't want to do nothing. Unwillingness is in a perpetual state of dissatisfaction so when they become the primary character running the show, there tends to be depression. We're going to learn how to work with unwillingness' wisdom to assess whether we really want to do something or not.

The Gift of Walking Away

"You never finish anything."

This is something I've heard so many times in my life. They usually came with variations such as "You're always so easily satisfied, you never go the extra mile." "Why don't you shoot for a 100%? Why are you always okay with 80%?" "You never give anything your full shot." Hearing this on so many different occasions, I naturally started believing this for myself: I never finish anything. I don't ever shoot for a 100%. I just don't put effort into anything.

Let's turn this idea that you're a non-finisher around on its head and celebrate it. How can I celebrate my suckiness, you might ask? Typically, something good becomes better the more you have it. Two bites of chocolate fudge cake is better than one bite. Two toys are better than one. A hundred dollars are better than a dollar.

Then comes this idea of diminishing returns. After a certain point, the more you do something - the appeal of it starts to decrease. Five bites of chocolate fudge is good but... twenty bites may be a bit nauseating. After about ten toys... your room slowly starts being a mess. After more than the amount of money you're comfortable with... you start feeling anxious about your money.

Being able to STOP at the point of diminishing returns gives you ALL the benefits with none of the down side. It's such a simple concept, right? Imagine being forced to eat all the food on the table but you enjoy NONE of the dishes. You're saving yourself from a torturous experience.

So by NOT finishing what you had no desire to finish, you're giving yourself the gift of preventing torment. You're giving yourself the gift of just the good parts of something. And you had this ability to gift to 2yourself innately... without anyone ever teaching you about this ability. How cool is that?

Unwillingness To Form

When you do an action, there has to be some parts you don't enjoy about it. That's why specialized tools and gear are in the market for almost everything. I used to use vertical mice for my computing environment in a previous job because I started to have wrist pains. The wrist pain comes with prolonged computer usage, but that doesn't mean I want to stop using the computer altogether. The computer is a big part of my livelihood and how I enjoy my time. It's just the current FORM of my computing that I don't want to continue.

Just like that, your unwillingness to do something may be a signal to change the FORM of how you are doing something. If you could have a writing career but spend less time writing... How would you be able to do that? There are lots of speech to text solutions available these days, so that could be a way to achieve that. You enjoy surfing but you don't like going to competitions... Maybe there are other ways to make surfing a profession, or I can work on competition mentality specifically instead of tying it to the joy of surfing.

Distinguishing whether your unwillingness is to the actual action or the form of the action can help the desire stay joyful. Here are some questions to make that distinction clearer:

- If I had no external pressure to do this task, would I still do it? (external pressure can be money, expected career trajectory, etc)
- If I completely removed this action from my life, what would I miss? What would I not miss?
- If I stop doing this, does it affect me the most or another person?
- What parts of your action would you recommend to a younger version of you, and what parts would you not recommend?

GUILT & SHAME

Guilt and shame, the dark curtain that hides us from being seen as our crappy self. Why do I even exist like this? Look at all the other people living their life fine. What's wrong with me? I can't be seen like this because I'm an embarrassment. This is what is always going through guilt and shame's mind. Guilt and shame always wants to hide and be disguised. The idea of being seen for who we are is their biggest fear. Why? We don't really know, all we know is that we're just that afraid.

Guilt and shame is the biggest contributor to inaction. In fact most of the reasons why our life does not go the way we want it to are related to guilt and shame. As such, they can be seen as the anti-hype. All the other characters in the ensemble have value and virtue because they are intelligent parts of you but guilt and shame, and specifically shame, has no place in a person's life who wants to live genuinely. I want you to envision shame like a ghost that lingers on in the physical plane because it has an unresolved wish (this is a concept called *han* in Korean culture). When you become genuinely you and free yourself from the need to invite shame into your life in the first place, shame can resolve its wish and happily move on to the spirit plane.

Shameless Hype

Remember when I said hype is a superhero who is almost too strong? Hype can not only work against shame, but hype can work with shame to resolve its *han*. Remember that shame enters into your life with an unresolved wish. That unresolved wish is the wish to be loved and accepted for who you are unconditionally.

Recall that shame always gives you perceived safety at the cost of joyful self-expression. For any shame you have around any aspect of you, there is something that is hidden by that shame. You may think you are ugly without hairdo and makeup; this masks your true self without anything on. You may think you are too lazy and unproductive; this masks your natural need for rest and revitalization.

When hype can work with shame to tell them "hey, I understand how afraid you are. I see that in the past you were shamed by others about something so innocent and carefree. I want to let you know that it's not you who did something wrong. The world is full of people with different opinions and unfortunately some of them believe you shouldn't be yourself. But there are others who would love to see you for who you are. Come on. Take my hand, we're going to see how great it is to finally be yourself!", shame finally understands what they wanted was acceptance AND authenticity.

Compassionate Witnessing

How hype talked to shame in the previous subchapter is an example of compassionate witnessing. Compassionate witnessing is a technique that is used to unshame ourselves. Every time you discover the root of a shameful feeling, there are two components: injury and shame.

The injury is when a negative event happens to the mind, causing it to receive damage. Like a physical injury, it can be the result of an accident or an attack; you can slip to have a broken hip, you can get punched by someone to have a concussion, and so on. Re-using the example from the section on perfectionism and shame, the injury is when the teacher looks at the drawing and sighs disapprovingly. Your drawing doesn't deserve that kind of treatment from anybody, but your teacher crosses the line and causes your mind to consider that this drawing is bad, what you created is bad.

Shame is what happens as a result of having *shaming* witnesses. This is different from *compassionate* witnessing. Suppose in the classroom, when the teacher made the disapproving remarks, your class burst into laughter and made fun of your drawing. Since that day you become the "crayon ruiner" and the "bad artist". These witnesses, the people who are not the ones that caused the initial injury, are the ones that open the doors for shame to enter into your life.

When you receive shame, whatever you may think about the injury gets silenced. You may think that your drawing is actually pretty good. You may be proud of how you used crayons for the first time. You may have followed some drawings you saw on YouTube and thought it was a good effort in trying what they did. But none of those matter, because in the end it's *bad*. Who cares what you thought? Everyone else in the world thinks it's bad. This suppression of your own voice makes you *less* you. Some people think that this kind of shame is necessary to make yourself fit into society. But that is not the truth because the truth is, you don't need to be anything. If fitting into society is the grand goal of everything, why do we celebrate rule-breakers? Why do so many people burn out trying to fit in? Why are so many people depressed to the point of suicidal ideations about their identity, if they're supposed to be happy when they conform to societal standards?

Compassionate witnessing is the type of witnessing that sees you for who you are and what you think. It is a friend who fights back to the teacher and the classmates, and proclaims: "Who are you to say that a drawing is good or bad? Your opinion is your opinion and it doesn't mean this drawing is bad!". It's the witnessing that reinforces your beliefs and your actions, and this kind of witnessing is what prevents and heals shame.

It is our job to be compassionate witnesses for ourselves, if we want to be truly self reliant. We have the ability to think of ourselves in first, second, and third persons. Utilizing that multiplicity of the mind and healing our shame by ourselves will lift the barrier in so many different aspects of your life that are not just limited to action. For a more in depth discussion about unshaming and how to do it to yourself, refer to my book "Own Your Cringe - How to be confident ABOUT your social anxiety".

Guilt and Shame As Part
of Perfection

In previous chapters we discussed your innate perfection and your inability to make bad decisions for yourself. (~) So seen in this way, guilt and shame are part of that perfection as well. This may seem contradictory because earlier I noted that shame has no place in a mentally healthy person's life. I still stand by that. What I mean in this chapter is, the *motivation* for keeping shame in your life is still noble.

You never consciously thought about the impact of shame in your life until you read these chapters. You wanted the best for yourself, so you wanted to follow established guidelines and best practices of how to live in the world. Underneath the negativity of shame is the desire to give yourself the best and nothing else. You did not intentionally invite shame into your life to ruin your mood and will for life.

When you do the work to unshame the beliefs that have held your life back, you will feel relief. The unshaming is lifting societal pressure so that you can be, respect, and listen to yourself more. If being you was supposed to be a bad thing and you actually needed to be bound by shame, then shouldn't unshaming feel bad? In my practice of unshaming and in other change workers' practice of unshaming, I have never encountered a person who felt worse as a result of unshaming. The comfort and permission to be yourself is a liberating, joyful experience.

As ironic as that sounds, without the experience of shame it can be difficult to fully appreciate the freedom and power to be just one hundred percent yourself. Viewed in this way, even your experience with guilt and shame was your life's way of building up to an explosive momentum of happiness and celebration.

ACTION IN PRACTICE

Now that you intimately know the characters inside of you, you can see how when you think about an action there will always be interactions among these characters about the action. For example let's say you're a passionate rock climber and you go to the climbing gym every day. The interaction would be something like:

Desire: Hey, I love climbing! There was a path I couldn't finish last time and I can't wait to try again!

Hype: Can you just see how fulfilling and satisfying it would be to finally land that final touch on the path? We've been struggling so much but when we tap on that final hold it'll all be worth it! Look at how much skill we've grown just by trying to get that path!

Perfectionism: I think you can work on some easier paths more, your technique isn't really THAT great, it's nothing to write home about. That's probably why you're not getting the difficult path.

Unwillingness: Can we just stay home? I don't like constantly being in muscle aches and sore fingers.

Guilt & Shame: I think perfectionism has a point... What would other people think when they see your crappy form? You're not that great, and-

Hype: HEYYY!!! I see all of your points, yes we have muscle aches yes we can be better but what matters right now is DESIRE WANTS TO TRY AGAIN! Isn't that right?

Desire: Yeah! I can definitely work on easier paths but today after listening to hype I just really want to try and get to that hold, GOSH I'm gonna feel SOOO HAPPY when I do!!!

Even if you don't narrate each character's voice, it's easy to see how when we're excited to do something no amount of unwillingness and perfectionism can override the excitement. But what if your excitement is low about something you HAVE to do?

> **Unwillingness**: I really don't want to pay taxes. I hate the paperwork, I hate looking at my finances, I hate this feeling of having deadlines...
>
> **Guilt & Shame**: Look at you. A full grown adult trying to run away from responsibilities. Why are you so irresponsible? If you were more likable maybe you'd have people helping you but look at you all alone, not able to do anything on your own.
>
> **Desire**: I'd really like the taxes to be done though, it'd be nice to not have to worry about penalties...
>
> **Hype**: Maybe we can even get a refund? Maybe we don't owe this year?
>
> **Perfectionism**: Are you stupid? The people who get refunds have had their financial life planned from day 0. We're comically late to being responsible it's almost pointless now. If only we started thinking about this when we just turned 18...
>
> **Guilt & Shame**: Yes... What were you even thinking at that time? What a disappointment you are. Just go scroll on your phone so you don't have to remind yourself of your failure.
>
> **Hype**: ... I'm gonna go somewhere else.
>
> **Desire**: But what about me?

The first example was a case of effortless action and the second was about energy sinks. Note how this characterization allows us to consider what each component would think about the action, instead of one of them taking over your mind and pretending that it is actually you thinking the thoughts.

Now, you have all the knowledge you need in order to fine-tune every parameter in your action life. Think of the action you've been putting off, and let's work with the parameters of the formula to get to effortless action or clean break.

Action Checklist

1. Do I want to do this action? What do I get out of this action? Why do I want to do it?
2. If it's completely fine to not want to do it, would I still want to do it?
3. If you answered No to both questions, congratulations! You can remove this from your life with a clean break!
4. If you answered yes, what's the smallest thing you can do related to this action?
5. What are the specific outcomes of this action, and what does that allow for my life?
   a. Preparing for interviews will give me job offers! A steady paycheck! A savings account!
   b. Weight loss will make me feel healthy! I won't be bloated all the time! I can invite more adventure to my life! I can enjoy more of the food I love!
   c. Social skills will invite more people to my life! I'll have more people to talk to! I'll be at more events! I'll hang out with more people!
6. What is the hype that I feel when I invite it to my body, using the technique in the hype chapter?
7. What are some side dish actions I want to incorporate along with this action so I can bounce back and forth, having fun?
8. What are some things that make me unwilling to do this action? Is there a way to address these pain points? Am I willing to accept these pain points as a cost for what I will get as a result of the action?
9. What is the smallest unit of believable action I can do related to this action?
10. Congratulations! If you answered these questions, actions are effortlessly streaming out of you!

This book is not only a suggestion of an idea to consider for your mind, but also living proof that this methodology works; I used this formula to write this book whenever I felt like not writing it! The formula has helped so many of my clients struggling with inaction, and I'm confident that it will help your actions too.

If you enjoyed this book, you'll also like my work on social anxiety called "Own Your Cringe: How to be confident ABOUT your social anxiety" available on Amazon https://www.amazon.com/dp/B0C7NL4H2D. To hire me as your life coach to overcome your struggles, explore the formula in action with the creator, or architect the life you want to live, email me at billy@julylifecoach.com to get started or get more information on my website https://www.julylifecoach.com/life-coaching-pricing. You can email me just to talk to me too, not just about coaching inquiries!

The artwork in this book is created by Riri Flawyi. She can be reached on Twitter https://twitter.com/ririflawyi, Instagram https://www.instagram.com/ririflawyi/, and email ririflawyi@gmail.com. Check out her portfolio here: https://ririflawyi.carrd.co/. For social media:

- I'm on Reddit as /u/julylifecoach.
- I'm on Instagram @july_lifecoach.
- I'm on YouTube as @julylifecoach.

I hope this book helped, and hope to continue the work on your life together.

Made in the USA
Coppell, TX
22 September 2023

21840624R00038